PROSPERITY

FOR

EVERYONE

Yes we can! … but how and when?

How to develop a clear overview, realistic goals,

optimism and self-reliance in our hectic world!

Walter Berger
Taschengeld Management

1st edition, was published in 2012, by Walter Berger,
Taschengeld Management, 83435 Bad Reichenhall, Germany

This is the 2nd edition of the book.

Please note: This book is also available as eBook and as audiobook.

English translation by Tansy Tazewell, Cologne www.tripl3t.de

Please note: For the English translation we used the English pages of
Wikipedia. There were sometimes differences in wording but we found
them quite appropriate and well suited.

EN-WBB-02
ISBN-13: 978-3-9814824-8-5

We all have the basic right to a fulfilled life!
That is far more than a brief victory in the daily struggle for
enough food, comfortable clothing, a warm house or an
inexpensive package holiday.
Walter Berger

CONTENTS

INTRODUCTION

ROY EUGENE DAVIS

DO EVERYTHING THAT SUPPORTS YOUR INTENTION TO BE PROSPEROUS. Harmoniously integrate the spiritual, mental, emotional, physical, social, vocational, recreational, economic, and environmental aspects of your life. Attend to your formal spiritual practices first.

Nurture optimism, confidence, and rational thinking. Be innovative and willing to learn. Imagine that you have what you need or want for your well-being. Remember that your mind is part of a universal mind that is responsive to your desires and intentions. Improve your powers of concentration and discrimination. Avoid pessimism, doubt, worry, and fantasy.

For emotional well-being, nurture calmness, soul-contentment, cheerfulness, and patience. Avoid restlessness, feelings of loneliness or hopelessness, anxiety, and insecurity.

For physical well-being, nurture your health with a positive mental attitude, nutritious foods (organic when possible), appropriate exercise, sufficient sleep and recreation, fresh air, and at least thirty minutes of daily exposure to natural light. (Full spectrum light helps the body's endocrine glands work efficiently.) Avoid mental states, moods, activities, and personal relationships that weaken or waste mental and physical energies.

For social harmony, relate to family members, friends, and others, express the virtues of compassion, kindness, generosity, and helpfulness. Avoid fault-finding, inclinations to control or dominate, and emotional dependency.

View your vocation as service and perform all actions skillfully. If you are not satisfied with the work you do, learn to do what will better utilize your knowledge and abilities. If you are temporarily out of work, affirm with conviction, "There is the right place in this world for me." Then discover or create it! Avoid laziness, procrastination, complacency, or boredom.

Playfully relax occasionally. Walk; swim; ride a bicycle; play tennis, golf, or croquet; take an ocean cruise or go boating on a river or lake; attend a music concert or a stage play; or do other things to refresh your mind and body.

Wisely manage and take care of material things. Regularly save some of your money and safely invest it for future needs. The guidelines provided by the author of this book will be very helpful. Have an attorney advise and help you draft a will that expresses your wishes regarding how you want your material things and money distributed after your demise.

Keep home and work areas clean. Recycle paper, plastic, metal, glass, and other no longer usable things. Conserve gas, electric power, water, and don't poison or damage the environment.

Choose thoughts, emotions, behaviours, relationships, activities, and environmental conditions that enhance your life and contribute to your total well-being. Avoid thoughts, moods, behaviours, relationships, activities, and environmental conditions which may be detrimental to your physical, psychological, and spiritual health. Doing that is easier than trying to remember a long list of things to do or to avoid.

Consider your life as an opportunity to be fully conscious of your true nature and live without limitations.

Roy Eugene Davis is the founder and director of Center for Spiritual Awareness with world headquarters in America and branches in several countries. He is a widely traveled speaker and the author of many books.

FOREWORD

How this workbook can help you, too!

"Prosperity is the state of flourishing, thriving, good fortune and/or successful social status. Prosperity often encompasses wealth but also includes others factors which are independent of wealth to varying degrees, such as happiness and health."
(http://en.wikipedia.org/wiki/Prosperity, 15 December 2011)

"TOO MUCH TIME FOR SUCH A SMALL AMOUNT OF MONEY!" Perhaps a little cynical, but a daily experience for many people. Life has become expensive and the money coming in often doesn't last until the end of the month. Rising costs and uncertain income lead to financial stress, physically and psychologically. Many may feel like "normal consumers" or "ordinary bill payers". Unfortunately they are rarely offered a liberating "haircut" or practical ways of reducing expenditure on a sustained basis. Every individual is responsible for getting a grip on their personal finances and mastering the challenges that face them every day.

But how? What is my financial situation really like and what can I do right now? What are the right decisions and how must I act now? The definition of "prosperity" (Wikipedia, see above) sounds great. But what are the prerequisites for prosperity and how is it possible to develop optimistic prospects that will also stand you in good stead in difficult situations?

This "work eBook" is a straightforward guide to help you to record your current financial situation in a structured way. You will be able to see the income you can reckon with more clearly, what you spend money on, which debts you have, what reserves are available to you, how you feel about the subject of money and finances or where you have or could have a problem.

You learn simple ways of reducing debts and creating reserves. You draw up a detailed income and expenditure budget and a current financial status.

At the end of every section you can write down important goals and milestones and decide what you want to achieve and how you should act now. This orientation will have a motivating effect on your everyday life and encourage you act consistently. Practical examples and easy-to-understand copy templates facilitate implementation in your day-to-day life.

Life is constant change and calls for continuous adjustment! An overview, knowledge, experience and intelligence enable good decisions to be made.

Good decisions that will stand you in good stead in the long term necessitate a good overview, knowledge, experience and intelligence. Trust in your own actions and in the further development support objectivity and composure, also when dealing with the flood of daily news. Disciplined action and appropriate adjustments are conducive to orientation in daily life and a prevailing mood of optimism as an important basis for a prosperous life.

Acción disciplinada y ajustes apropiados son propicios para la orientación en la vida diaria y un estado de ánimo predominante de optimismo como una base importante para una vida próspera.

Please don't forget that this is a "work eBook" and not an entertaining novel to escape from reality for a moment! Start by reading the list of contents and then work through the individual sections. Sit down somewhere where you will not be disturbed. The documents you need should be at hand. Highlight and underline important passages and make your own notes. Take enough time and answer all the questions honestly and in full – especially the unpleasant ones. Start right now!

And another tip: Please don't tell anyone about your decision and your plan. They'll only discuss it to death! You might need to justify your decision or even defend it. Then you could soon lose your motivation and you might subconsciously prepare excuses for situations where dealing with things becomes uncomfortable.

Just do it because you think it makes sense right now!

It is helpful to plan a certain time each day to work through the book. If certain questions cannot be answered immediately, simply move onto the next part. All the individual results will create a larger picture that will make your current situation clear and show you what the right steps are to take next. The whole is more than the sum of its parts!

The Book is also available in printed form as an eBook or as an audiobook. Many examples are shown crossways. The landscape format helps you to see the whole picture and makes it easier to understand how things are connected and related. This can stimulate creativity for new ideas and present surprising solutions. At the end of the book you will find neutral examples for your personal use. Compile a valuable source for important financial and personal decisions.

Start right now and make your personal workbook!

We all have the basic right to a fulfilled life. That is far more than a brief victory in the daily struggle for enough food, comfortable clothing, a warm house or an inexpensive package holiday.

Walter Berger, Taschengeld Management

1 CASH CHECK

A little fire is quickly trodden out,

which being suffr'd, rivers cannot quench!

William Shakespeare, Henry VI.

The aim of a cash check is to determine the cash balance.

IMAGINE, IT'S MONDAY MORNING, at the start of a new long and hard working week, near the end of the month and the money. Last weekend the club was unmotivated and lost a boring home game. The other team was a little better and luckier for that day. It's grey and it's raining. Today there's no point hoping for a bit of sun. There – a smile! He's sure to want something from me! Do you know that kind of mood?

It's an ideal time to examine your own frame of mind and attitudes and those of others. Ask the following questions on such a day: "How are you?" or "What are you doing?" and then listen carefully to the answers.

Complaining, illnesses, poring over problems, looking for the guilty party, the latest crises, cynicism, aggressiveness or successes, plans, opportunities, joy, a good mood, a smile, laughter. Listen to the answers and observe the reactions. You'll find out a lot about thoughts, attitudes, fixations, conditioning, about positive or negative moods and about what moves people, drives them and makes them react.

Avoid superficial conversations and destructive information from the media. Simply continue, switch off and don't read the latest version of "Give us this day our daily problem!". Don't take everything personally! Negative moods and ideas are catching and it's difficult to get rid of them again. They stick to you for a long time and follow you in your sleep. Stay positive and realistic!

This section gives you an opportunity to do an emotional "cash check". How are you? Are you content, optimistic and well-adjusted? What do you do? How do you occupy yourself and what worries you? How do you feel and what's really up? What's the problem and what would the ideal situation be?

Take a look at your life! Describe your current situation vividly. What emotions come up? What do you think and feel? Write it down and get it all off your chest! What do you really want? Be specific! What would an ideal situation be like? What will it be like when it becomes reality? How will you feel?

Everything is temporary!
But some things just take a little longer!
Roy Eugene Davis

How are you?
Emotional "cash check"

Describe your current situation (personal, professional, financial etc.) and allow yourself to be guided by the following questions.

- How satisfied am I with this situation? What is good and pleasing?
- What troubles me? What makes me angry? What stresses me?
- How did the current situation come about? What are the causes?
- How will my situation develop, in the next 6 months and in the next 5 years?
- What advantages and what disadvantages this development will have?
- What would an ideal situation be like?
- What could I do to be really happy and content?
- WHAT WILL I DO? HOW DO I SOLVE THE PROBLEM? WHAT IS NECESSARY?

My notes: My calculations:

*If you want to be taken seriously,
then take yourself seriously first!*

2 EXPENDITURE

I am rich because I can pay all my outgoings!

The term "expenditure" is looked at under two aspects in this section:

1.   The act of spending money, i.e. how and why money is spent.

2.   The type of expenditure, i.e. what is bought or what money is spent on.

SOME TIME AGO THE TV STATION ARTE broadcast an interesting film entitled "Ich kaufe, also bin ich" ("I buy therefore I am"). It was shown that on average a US citizen consumes approximately 25,000 commercials per year. 25,000 times is not only a product presented to the viewer, but also a scale of values and an attitude to life. Superficial stimuli target deep-seated needs and anxieties and try to arouse a desire to buy – with big success.

In the past the main advertising message was "Buy this or that and then you can keep up and will be popular!" Today the predominant message is "Buy that and then you'll be happy!" Today 20 times more money is spent on children's advertising than in 1980.

Do you always make conscious and rational buying decisions when you do your daily supermarket shopping, when you see clothes on special offer, amazing bargains, when you buy a new car or when you plan your next dream holiday? Do you only buy the things you need that are on your shopping list, or do you sometimes make impulse buys or even buy things out of frustration? Do you often treat yourself when shopping? When looking through your wardrobe do you sometimes wonder "Why did I buy that?" or worse "Who bought this?".

Use this section to reflect on your consumer behaviour, without assigning blame and without trying to justify strange buying decisions in retrospect. Gain an overview of your expenditure to date. This will show you how much money you have spent on what in the past. You will see what your basic needs are and how much money you spend on maintaining the lifestyle you love. Get to know yourself a little better and then decide yourself where your spending priorities lie.

If you follow the herd you'll end as a meat chop!

What do I spend money on?

Write down what you spent money on last month.

- How much money did you spend on each type of expenditure?

- What were the necessary living expenses?

- What percentage of your total expenditure is assigned to each type of spending?

Type of expenditure	€	Really necessary? yes/no	%

If you don't know where your money disappears to…

… here's a way to find out!

- Write down everything you spend money on.

  Make sure that everything is covered.

  All information is important!

- Pay for everything with cash if possible.

- Avoid paying with credit cards or checks if possible.

- Collect all receipts and sort them by date.

- Once a week write down all your expenditure in a cash book or a journal.

- Identify types of expenditure and set priorities.

Use this expenditure journal for your wallet:

My expenditure				
Date	Amount	What	Payment method	Priority
Priorities: A = necessary, B = important, C = pleasant, D = unnecessary				

Get to know yourself a bit better!

An overview of my expenditure

To get an overview of your expenditure proceed as follows:

1. Collect, order and list receipts and bank statements.

2. Record all cash expenditure (see previous page).

3. Identify types of expenditure, e.g. rent, food, electricity, telephone, insurance, car etc.

4. How much do you spend on each type of expenditure per month?

5. What annual payments were made?

6. Examine each type of expenditure in terms of the amount and necessity.

7. Set priorities (what is important to you?).

8. Set a monthly budget for each type of expenditure. (Monthly payment and 1/12 of the annual sum (if available) gives you the figure to be set.)

Example for creating an overview of your expenditure:

EXPENDITURE	Spent each month so far	Annual, urgent, extraordinary needs	Monthly budget	Priority
Rent	€365.00		€365.00	A
Additional expenses	€65.00	€170.00	€79.17	A
Electricity	€59.00	€160.00	€72.33	A
Food	€250.00		€250.00	A
Clothing	€50.00		€50.00	B
Hairdresser	€15.00		€15.00	B
Telephone / Mobile	€25.00		€25.00	B
Personal liability insurance		€35.00	€2.92	A
...				
Total expenditure/month	€829.00	€365.00	€859.42	

NOTES on my expenditure:

Where is there an urgent need to take action? What will I do?

My calculations:

My notes:

3 INCOME

How much must I earn?

"...for households and individuals, "income is the sum of all the wages, salaries, profits, interests payments, rents and other forms of earnings received... in a given period of time." (http://en.wikipedia.org/wiki/Income, 11. November 2011)

"I AM NOW A BENEFIT RECIPIENT!" said an old friend with a wide grin. When I enquired he added that he had entered well-deserved retirement a few weeks ago. Are you also a recipient of benefits or do you earn your money? Would you employ yourself and how much would you pay yourself? Is your work, the service or the product for your company or your customers worth considerably more than has to be paid for it?

It can be painful, but certainly very useful and sometimes beneficial to honestly ask yourself these questions. "Is it (still) worth it?" Your employer and especially your customers must ask themselves this essential question every day. You would do the same in their place, wouldn't you?

There is no guarantee of long-term employment with secure remuneration and a generous pension plan. The successful principle for good chances on the labour market, a secure job or flourishing sales is simple: My work or my product should be worth considerably more for my company or my customers than they have to pay for it and they should be aware of it.

But take care: If you focus exclusively on the best monetary value you'll soon become a cheap jack. This often leads to cutthroat price and discount wars and cultivates a competitive, aggressive and negative climate. In the end no one feels like a winner. The boss thinks: "My staff are too expensive, I pay them too much."

The employee thinks: "What a pittance, I'm being exploited." The buyer might think: "I could have got even more out of it" and the seller feels peeved that he was not adequately paid for his work.

Place the focus more strongly on the utility value, the benefits, the advantages and the possibilities for your company and your customers. Present yourself as a provider of solutions! A creative and positive mood creates long-term satisfaction. You are a person people like working with. Follow-up orders are the norm!

How much can I earn?

Are you worried about the security of your job? Then examine the situation with the following questions: Who needs my work? Can someone else do it more cheaply or quickly? Are there better alternatives? How do my work and my services benefit my company or my customers? What is my company lacking to be/stay competitive? How is my company's range of products developing? Will this affect my work or my job? What additional added value can I offer?

If you are currently looking for a job you should be aware of the benefits you can offer the company in question. If you yourself are convinced and are able to show this, then you have a good chance to convince others!

In the previous section you compiled an overview of your expenditure. You now have more clarity about how much money you spent in the past and what you spent it on. Spending priorities (A, B, C, ...) facilitate a division into essential basic needs right through to frustration-motivated purchases. If it becomes necessary to make savings in future it will then be much easier to make wise decisions.

The amount of total expenditure shows you how much your previous lifestyle and each individual type of expenditure has cost you. If you do not want to make any major changes to this you can use the totals as a planning basis for the expenditure budget. Please note that price increases or unexpected expenditure are not considered in this!

In this section you will establish what income you have had to date and how much money you can reckon with. The amount of future income should be estimated realistically. You examine your income to date in detail in order to identify ways of improving your current income situation.

Making an income prediction is a simple matter for employees as they have a wage or salary guaranteed in a contract.
However, it is also important to examine variable elements of the remuneration (extra pay, bonuses etc.) in terms of reliability and plannability.

This is a little more difficult for people who are self-employed. Their living expenses come from the profit made from their work or from reserves. Here, the estimated future income is much more speculative, because the future revenue is not yet earned and costs, taxes and social insurance contributions also not yet paid. It therefore makes sense to set the expected annual private expenditure as the minimum profit and to calculate the minimum turnover needed from this.

**A careful assessment of future income
enables realistic planning!**

How much have you earned in your life so far?

- Write down all positions and jobs you have held (including holiday jobs, temporary jobs etc.)

- How much money did you earn in each job?

- How did you get the job? (Use a further page if you need to)

What work:	Money earned: €	How/from whom did you find about this job?
Total:	Σ	

Would you employ yourself and how much would you pay yourself?

- What is your present job and how much money do you earn?

- Where does your monthly income come from?

- What do your job security and the length of your employment contract depend on?

My notes: My calculations:

Example for creating an overview of your income:

INCOME	Current monthly earnings	Special payments, bonus etc.	Monthly budget	Secure income?
Employment	€1,480.00		€1,480.00	yes
Holiday pay		€600.00		no
Christmas bonus		€160.00		no
Child benefit	€328.00		€328.00	yes
Total income month	€1,808.00	€760.00	€1,808.00	

A close-up look at my income

Please examine your job and your planned income with the following questions:

- Do you like your job? Do you like what you do?

- How do you feel when you think about your job, especially on Sunday afternoon or Monday morning?

- How secure is your job and the amount of your income?

- What are any special payments dependent on in future?

- Could you manage financially with less income or even losing your job?

- For how long?

- What ongoing costs are incurred by your job? (petrol, car, train, etc.)

- Are there further opportunities for generating income? What are they?

- Are there better job offers?

My notes: My calculations:

Uncertain income leads to financial stress!

NOTES on my income:

Where is there an urgent need to take action? What will I do?

My notes: My calculations:

4 RESERVES

"An asset is a resource controlled by the entity as a result of past events and from which future economic benefits are expected to flow to the entity."
(http://en.wikipedia.org/wiki/Asset, 28 December 2011)

"Simply stated, assets represent ownership of value that can be converted into cash (although cash itself is also considered an asset)."
(http://en.wikipedia.org/wiki/Asset, 28 December 2011)

BEING WEALTHY AND SOLVENT ARE NOT THE SAME THING! At the beginning of 2011 a TV documentary showed Americans who had lost their job in the financial crisis and were now homeless. The shocking thing was that they were living in their almost new luxury cars that no one wanted to buy anymore. One family interviewed had parked their caravan in friends' garden. One man had his little daughter on his lap and wearily described his daily battle to get enough food.

RESERVES ARE ESSENTIAL. A squirrel who stockpiles for the winter acts instinctively. And humans, too, have always stocked up on food for emergencies or bad times. Food, water, oil, energy (albeit to a limited extent) and much more are still kept as civil emergency reserves. The key question for the amount and the necessity of reserves is always: "If I can no longer have this or that from today onwards, or this is not anymore available because of any reason, for how long can I keep going and survive?" This should be the most important motivation and goal for not spending everything but putting something aside for "hard times".

Do you have sufficient reserves? Could you get by on less income? Could you cope with losing your job over a longer period without major financial problems? Are expensive repairs a particular problem? How quickly would financial reserves be available without major losses?

Liquid reserves are an important key to staying capable of financial action. In this section you compile an asset status, i.e. a detailed overview of your current assets. A particular focus is on liquid reserves and quick availability for acute emergencies. Liquid reserves to cover ongoing expenses for at least 6 months would be ideal. We will show you an intelligent way of apportioning your income. The aim is to pay ongoing expenses, build up reserves and repay debts.

Stay consistent and disciplined and build up sufficient liquid reserves!

*What's the point in having a great car
if I can't afford the petrol?*

"When I earn enough I'll start saving!"

Please enter all positions and jobs you have held to date again here (cf. section on income).

- How much have you earned in your life in total?

- What is left?

What work:	Total earned:	Left over today:
Total:	Σ	Σ

... but how much is enough to start?

"What value do my assets have for others?"

Use this page to create an overview of your assets (continue on further pages if necessary).

Enter all your assets according to type and value. Create an inventory!

List all your "treasures" and estimate their actual value today.

Be honest, if you wanted to sell it today how much would someone really pay you for it?

Asset/object:	Purchase price?	Value today? €	How liquid is the asset?
Total:	Σ	Σ	

Deep in our brain we still have a predisposition to hunting and gathering.
But the type of hunting and the prey have changed.

Intelligent income distribution

Find out about it here: (Pay attention to the order!)

- Start regularly saving 10% of your income now!

    o The goal is to have 6 times your monthly expenditure available as liquid resources (CASH). Use the totals and the compound interest by regularly saving 10% of all income you receive.

    o Lots of a little is a lot!

    o For liquid reserves the interest rate offered should not be decisive as higher interest usually entails a higher risk of loss or expensive termination costs.
    Avoid moving to speculative currencies. If the money is needed it must be exchanged, whatever the exchange rate!

    o Constant quick availability without major losses is important.

- A maximum of 90% of your income should be used for expenditure and payment of instalments (debts).

    o You might need to cut expenses.

    o Negotiate better terms with your creditors.

- Use additional income to pay off debts more quickly!

- Plan to save regular amounts and create reserves for larger purchases.

Example of intelligent income distribution:

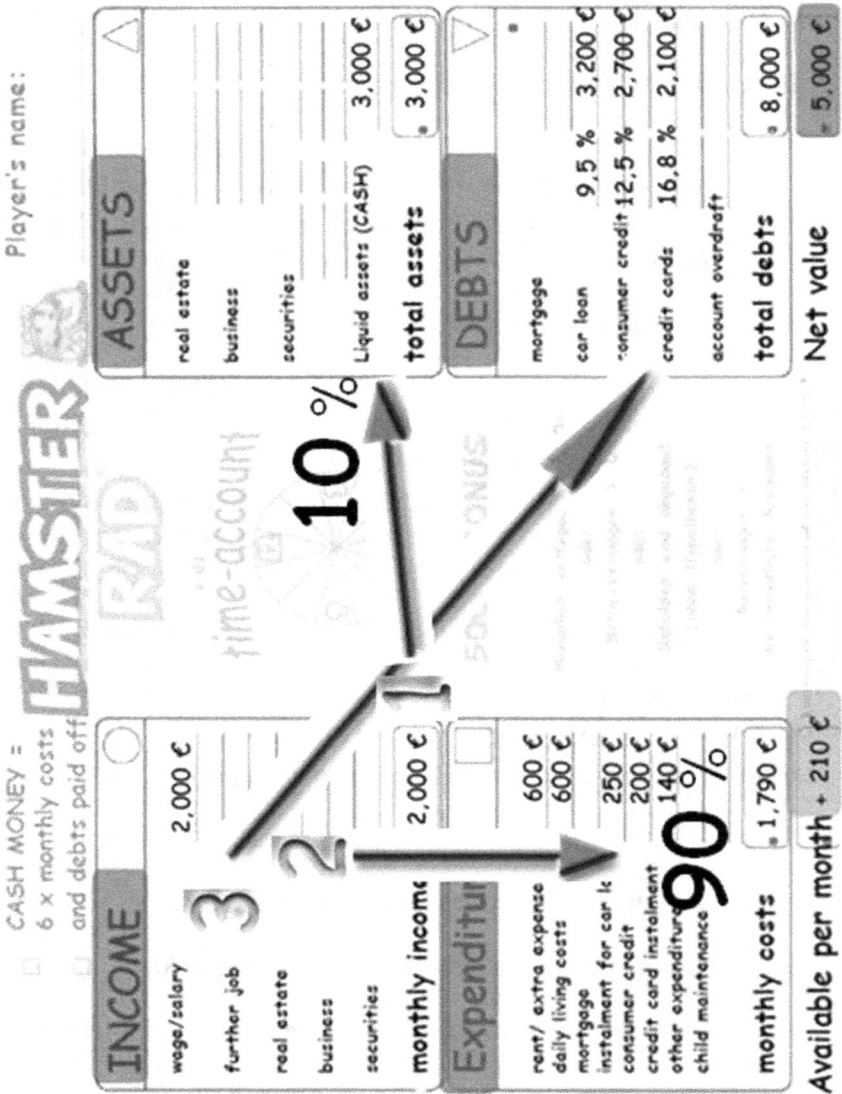

Player's name:

CASH MONEY =
6 x monthly costs
and debts paid off

HAMSTER

RAD

time-account

INCOME

wage/salary	2,000 €
further job	
real estate	
business	
securities	
monthly income	**2,000 €**

Expenditure

rent/ extra expense	600 €
daily living costs	600 €
mortgage	
instalment for car loan	250 €
consumer credit	200 €
credit card instalment	140 €
other expenditure	
child maintenance	
monthly costs	**1,790 €**

90 %

10 %

1

2

3

ASSETS

real estate	
business	
securities	
Liquid assets (CASH)	3,000 €
total assets	**3,000 €**

DEBTS

mortgage		
car loan	9,5 %	3,200 €
consumer credit	12,5 %	2,700 €
credit cards	16,8 %	2,100 €
account overdraft		
total debts		**8,000 €**

Net value 5,000 €

Available per month + 210 €

1. Save 10% (cash!)

2. Spend max. 90% on outgoings, debts, reserves

3. Use additional income to reduce debts

NOTES on my reserves:

Where is there an urgent need to take action? What will I do?

My calculations:

My notes:

5 DEBTS

Debts = Energy needed for tomorrow

that was already used yesterday.

"A debt is an obligation owed by one party (the debtor) to a second party, the creditor; usually this refers to assets granted by the creditor to the debtor, but the term can also be used metaphorically to cover moral obligations and other interactions not based on economic value.

A debt is created when a creditor agrees to lend a sum of assets to a debtor. Debt is usually granted with expected repayment; in modern society, in most cases, of the original sum plus interest.

In finance, debt is a means of using anticipated future purchasing power in the present before it has actually been earned. Some companies and corporations use debt as a part of their overall corporate finance strategy."

(http://en.wikipedia.org/wiki/Debt, 04 January 2012)

AT THE BEGINNING OF November 2011 several residents of a village outside Peking, China were interviewed. The reporter wanted to capture the sentiments of rural Chinese on the massive debts that many foreign states have to China. With a twinkle in his eye one man approached said: "The Europeans are greedy for meat! They do everything to get more meat. When they don't have any money they borrow money to get even more meat. We love meat as well. But when we don't have any money we don't buy any meat!" This comment might sound fatuous at first and perhaps say something about the value of meat for this man. But when the word "meat" is replaced by "consumption" you soon see the deeper truth:

In Europe we live beyond our means and pay with money that we do not have!

China has considerable foreign exchange reserves, maybe also because gushing tax income is not necessarily used to expand basic social services for all sections of the population. One reason for the strong economic growth and the high profits in connection with this are the extremely low labour costs, usually at the expense of the working population, who often have to get by on extremely low wages. This favourable time is used for buying and making worldwide investments in the expansion of trade relations, key markets and in securing the energy and raw material resources needed. Today, many countries are battling with dramatic liquidity problems and have huge debts to China!

Not guilty!

"How about a little more?" Making debts is easy. "Treat yourself, you've earned it!" A tempting offer, convenient payment in instalments, a real bargain. Stores entice us with slogans such as "I'm not stupid!" You can buy it on credit. You have credit!

"I don´t blame you. …You can believe in me … Trust in me!" sang the snake Ka to Mogli in The Jungle-Book. (You will find nice movies on YouTube!)

But it would be too easy to denounce manipulative advertising, profit-oriented companies, greedy banks, politicians who want to be re-elected or even fate as the guilty seducer and to absolve ourselves as will-less victims.

Responsible action also means responsibility to accept the consequences. A person has financial debts when they have bought something on credit. Perhaps the reason for an unpleasant situation today was a short-sighted decision in the past. It is not worth looking for someone to blame or feeling guilty. This only robs us of additional energy. There is a difficult situation that now needs to be resolved wisely. You cannot reverse what you have done, but you can learn from it and move on and act in a better way.

Oppressive debts and high monthly instalments disappear when you pay them off and do not take on any new ones!

This might sound simple, but it calls for emotional balance, a realistic overview of your financial situation and possible options for action, resolve and discipline.

This section will give you clarity about your existing debts and liabilities. You learn 8 steps to reduce debts. You draw up a debt cancellation plan and obtain a good overview in order to set payment priorities. It then becomes easier to identify positive progress towards the goal of "freedom from debt".

Oppressive debts and monthly instalments disappear when you pay them off and do not take on any new ones!

Fear as a motivator and loss of capacity to act

Answer the following questions here:

- To whom do I owe money?

- Why? What did I buy?

- What monthly repayments do I have to make for this?

- When will I be free of debts?

- How do I feel?

My notes: My calculations:

8 steps to freedom from debt (part 1)

Proceed as follows to draw up a debt cancellation plan and to pay off your debts:

1. Enter all debts in the "debt cancellation plan".
    (Please use the copy templates in the appendix for this.)

2. Decide on your ranking list for repaying existing debts, e.g.

    a. pay off the loan with the highest rate of interest first
       or

    b. the smallest loan (fast positive results motivate!) or

    c. the shortest repayment time (and there's another debt paid off!)

3. Negotiate better terms with your creditors. Talk about

    a. possibilities for agreeing a lower rate of interest or possible debt restructuring (overdrawing a current account is very expensive!), about

    b. lower monthly instalments or about

    c. partial debt cancellation, i.e. a "compounding arrangement". This means that the whole debt is redeemed upon payment of a partial amount.

Take action! You'll be amazed at what can be achieved by talking and staying on the ball!

Example of a debt cancellation plan:

My debt cancellation plan

What debt? creditor	Current amount	Current rate of interest	Minimum instalment /month	No. of instalments /month	Offer from creditor	Rate of interest new	Instalment /month new	No. of instalments /month new	Order of priority
Car purchase	€5,800	6.4 %	€151.77	28	Purchase		€0.00		4
Current account	€2,350	12.8 %	€25.07	never	Debt restructuring	9.4 %	€75.00	35	1
Bedroom	€2,700	9.8 %	€134.55	23	Reduction €1.800	9.8 %	€114.70	15	3
Credit card	€1,250	18.4 %	€31.67	60	Better interest rate, repay more	12.4 %	€31.67	50	2
Debts/ monthly payments	€12,100		€343.06				€221.37		

8 steps to freedom from debt (part 2)

4. Transfer the monthly instalments to the expenditure budget.

5. If necessary, reduce your expenditure and generate additional income.

6. Start regularly saving 10% of your income right now! Give it a try! You'll see that it can be done if you want it.

7. Pay the agreed instalments regularly and on time.

    a. Use any additional income for higher repayment of the current number 1 on your debt ranking list.

    b. When one debt has been paid off, tackle the next one!

    c. Use the liquidity released from the debt paid off to pay off the next debt more quickly.

    d. Proceed in this way until all debts have been paid off.

8. Once all debts have been paid off you should aim to save liquid reserves of up to 6 times your monthly expenditure.

Congratulation! You have credit again! Please don't use it!

Reduce your debts and create reserves –
both are possible!

NOTES on my debts:

Where is there an urgent need to take action? What will I do?

My calculations:

My notes:

6 PURCHASES

"Fulfil a wish!", the sirens sing!
Fulfilling endless wishes becomes the purpose in life,
"more and more" is the goal,
"being content with less" means "failing".
What wishes do I have (get) today?

"Consumption is a common concept in economics, and gives rise to derived concepts such as consumer debt. Generally, consumption is defined in part by comparison to production. But the precise definition can vary because different schools of economists define production quite differently. According to mainstream economists, only the final purchase of goods and services by individuals constitutes consumption, while other types of expenditure — in particular, fixed investment, intermediate consumption and government spending — are placed in separate categories. Other economists define consumption much more broadly, as the aggregate of all economic activity that does not entail the design, production and marketing of goods and services (e.g. the selection, adoption, use, disposal and recycling of goods and services)."

(http://en.wikipedia.org/wiki/Consumption_%28economics%29, 04 January 2012)

A LITTLE GIRL IS TALKING TO HER FRIEND ABOUT THE FINANCIAL CRISIS. "We're really poor now! Now my dad can only afford a car without a roof!" and she points to a brand-new cabriolet parked in the drive.

It's wonderful to have dreams. It is satisfying to fulfil wishes and to be able to afford to give others presents or

45

support them financially. Trust in the future and a healthy consciousness of prosperity promote private consumption. Companies, jobs and tax income depend on this.

However, spontaneous purchases, special promotions, one-off bargains, sensational opportunities, frustration or impulse buys should be avoided. They only lead to spending too much money and perhaps not having sufficient funds available for emergencies. Be honest: when you look in your wardrobe do you see anything that can be assigned to the category of impulse buys or that was bought cheaply, put away and forgotten?

Larger investments and expensive purchases should be planned. The necessity, financial means and consequences should be scrutinised. What do I want to afford? What can I afford? Can I afford it later as well?

In this section you can write down all larger purchases that you are planning. It is a good opportunity to discuss wishes and plans with your partner or family and to take all ideas and suggestions seriously.

Discuss what is important to every individual, what should have priority, what you can afford and find out what investments are not (yet) possible. Is there something that you will have to do without? How much should you put aside each month? Make a joint decision and then go ahead!

What do I want to (can I) afford?

Here you can write down the dreams and wishes that you would like to fulfil.

- What do I want to buy?

- What investments or purchases are planned?

Please answer the questions as precisely as possible, i.e.:
What? When? How expensive? Why? How will you feel then?

My notes: My calculations:

Example for creating an overview of purchases:

WISHES/PURCHASES/INVESTMENTS				
	How expensive?	When?	Monthly amount to be saved:	Necessary ?
Holiday	€1,500.00	August 12	€200.00	B
Car	€7,500.00	July 13	€150.00	B
Monthly reserves for purchases/investments:			€350.00	

A close-up look at my purchases

Please examine your planned purchases honestly with the
following questions:

- Why do I need it?

- Is it really necessary?

- Does it have to be so big, so …?

- Are there cheaper alternatives?

- If means a big investment, sleep on it!

- Avoid impulse buys.

- What would happen if I don't buy it?

My notes: My calculations:

I buy therefore I am. I am what I buy. What are you really?

Set realistic goals and find a way of making them come true!

Where is there an urgent need to take action? What will I do?

My calculations:

My notes:

7 BUDGET

Budget: A budget is a financial plan showing income and

expenditure to be expected in future.

I ONLY BUY WHAT I CAN AFFORD. I always have €50 more than I need in my wallet. Do you know similar, surely well-meant pieces of advice? These are usually no use at all in your everyday life. Rising prices, unforeseen expenses, urgent repairs, the loss of extra pay or the cancellation of a bonus you had reckoned with are difficult to plan. This makes it all the more important to always have an up-to-date overview of your income and expenditure so that you can react sensibly and flexibly to unpleasant surprises.

A tip: Make a full list of all your expenditure and plan reserves! Estimate your income realistically without considering bonuses, special payments etc. Surprising additional income is better than a big hole in your finances due to an overly optimistic estimate.

In this section you draw up an income and expenditure budget, i.e. you establish planned future expenditure and the income you expect. Follow the recommended steps and transfer all the results so far into the areas provided in the budget.

The individual parts of the puzzle create your financial map!

Take care! A budget is a plan based on past values and with assumptions for the future. The target provides a good orientation, although it must be continuously updated with the actual figures. Your plan must prove itself in reality. In this way the need to take action and possible options can be identified in appropriate time.

Stay realistic – create reserves!

Budget (part 1/expenditure)

An overview shows where action is needed and the possible options.

To draw up a plan proceed as follows:

- Enter the figures ascertained from the sections Expenditure, Debts and Purchases. (Please use the copy template in the appendix for this.)

    - 1/12 of your annual income is set as a monthly figure in the budget.

    - Don't underestimate your expenditure and consider possible price increases for heating, food, electricity, petrol etc.

- Enter the monthly instalments for the repayment of existing debts.

- Plan 10% of your income for building up liquid reserves.

- Consider amounts you save for planned purchases (holiday, car, furniture, etc.).

- Compare your actual expenditure with the figures in the budget every week (actual/target analysis). Deviations are identified in good time and necessary adjustments can be made.

Start acting at last instead of always reacting!

Example for creating an expenditure budget:

Budget	Monthly	Annually	Excess/Shortfall	Jan	Feb	Mar	Apr	May
Private expenditure								
Rent (including heating)	€ 365	€ 1,380		€ 365	€ 365	€ 365	€ 365	€ 365
Additional expenses	€ 79	€ 1,288		€ 79	€ 79	€ 79	€ 79	€ 79
Electricity	€ 72	€ 1,184		€ 72	€ 72	€ 72	€ 72	€ 72
Child maintenance								
Repayment								
Food	€ 230	€ 3,000		€ 230	€ 230	€ 230	€ 230	€ 230
Clothing	€ 50	€ 600		€ 50	€ 50	€ 50	€ 50	€ 50
Hairdresser	€ 15	€ 180		€ 15	€ 15	€ 15	€ 15	€ 15
Tel / mobile	€ 25	€ 300		€ 25	€ 25	€ 25	€ 25	€ 25
Liability insurance	€ 3	€ 35		€ 3	€ 3	€ 3	€ 3	€ 3
Total private expenditure	€ 859	€ 10,967		€ 859	€ 859	€ 859	€ 859	€ 859
Debts								
Car purchase								
Overdraft charges	€ 24	€ 291		€ 24	€ 24	€ 24	€ 24	€ 24
Bedroom	€ 113	€ 1,350		€ 113	€ 113	€ 113	€ 113	€ 113
Credit card	€ 50	€ 605		€ 50	€ 50	€ 50	€ 50	€ 50
Total debts	€ 187	€ 2,246		€ 187	€ 187	€ 187	€ 187	€ 187
Total income – debts	€ 1,046	€ 13,213	0	€ 1,046	€ 1,046	€ 1,046	€ 1,046	€ 1,046

57

Budget (part 2/income)

Careful assumptions for realistic planning

To draw up a budget proceed as follows:

1. Enter the figures ascertained from the Income section in your budget. (Please use the copy template in the appendix for this.)

    - 1/12 of your annual income is set as a monthly figure in the budget.

    - Stay realistic!

2. Do not plan with high one-off payments and variable parts of your employment contract such as Christmas or other bonuses and extra pay.

3. Financial reserves give you additional scope!

4. At least once a month compare your actual income with the figures in the budget (actual/target analysis). Establish the reasons for any differences and whether this is a one-off situation or if it will continue.

5. In the event of a shortfall examine the possible options: Use reserves, reduce your expenditure, find an additional job etc. Avoid overdrawing your account (very expensive) or paying with credit cards.

The best plan is worthless if it is not followed consistently!

Example for creating an income budget:

Budget	Monthly	Annually	Excess/Shortfall	Jan	Feb	Mar	Apr	May
Income								
Employment	€ 2,000	€ 24,000		€ 2,000	€ 2,000	€ 2,000	€ 2,000	€ 2,000
Holiday pay		€ 600		€ 0	€ 0	€ 0	€ 0	€ 0
Christmas bonus		€ 240		€ 0	€ 0	€ 0	€ 0	€ 0
Child benefit	€ 328	€ 3,936		€ 328	€ 328	€ 328	€ 328	€ 328
				€ 0	€ 0	€ 0	€ 0	€ 0
Total income	€ 2,328	€ 28,776	0	€ 2,328	€ 2,328	€ 2,328	€ 2,328	€ 2,328

NOTES on my budget:

Where is there an urgent need to take action? What will I do?

My calculations:

My notes:

8 FINANCIAL STATUS

A picture says more than a thousand words!

A financial status will give you a current overview of your income, expenditure, assets and debts. The financial status from the HAMSTERRAD® game is used to illustrate this.

A WOMAN REFLECTED ON HER FINANCIAL STATUS AND SIGHED: "It's like in real life! The only difference is that problems and the way that things are linked can be seen more easily." Her husband looked at her in agreement and confirmed: "That's what I always wanted to explain to you!"

"My daughter wants to show you something!" On the 3rd day of the games fair in Essen a man came up to me with his daughter and greeted me warmly. The girl grinned at me, rummaged around in her sweatshirt, pulled out a crumpled piece of paper and tried to smooth it out. "I beat my dad in the game yesterday!" she said triumphantly. And to prove it she handed me the financial status from the game HAMSTERRAD®.

"Can I take my financial status home with me?" Following a games evening a young woman asked this as she held a piece of paper out towards me. I looked at her a little surprised and answered: "Of course you can, but wouldn't you prefer to take a new sheet with you?" -

"No, thank you, this plan is sufficient. I just want to show my husband that I can manage money as well!" was the surprising answer.

Don't you also enjoy listening to an exceptionally gifted speaker who is able to explain even the most complex interrelations seemingly effortlessly in a simple and clear way? Have you ever tried to explain a complex issue so that it is really understood?

Can't you see the wood for the trees sometimes in the daily information jungle?

In the Financial status section you draw up a "financial map". Your financial situation and the way that things are linked become clearer. This overview makes it easier to identify necessary steps and sensible courses of action.

On just a single sheet of paper you can reason, discuss and decide instead of giving up in frustration with thousands of files, documents and figures.

*Learn to see things as they really are and
not as we imagine they are!
Vernon Howard*

Procedure for creating a financial status (part 1 income/expenditure):

1. Transfer the monthly figures from the budget (income / expenditure) to the financial status.

2. If necessary, combine individual expenses in categories.

3. Enter the monthly instalments for debts in the list of expenses.

4. Calculate totals for income and expenditure.

5. Ascertain how much money is available each month, or if there is a shortfall.

INCOME

- wage/salary
- further job
- real estate
- business
- securities

monthly income

Expenditure

- rent/ extra expenses
- daily living costs
- mortgage
- instalment for car loan
- consumer credit
- credit card instalm
- other expenditure
- child maintenance

monthly costs

Available per month

What you can see here:

- What income and expenditure do I have?

- What is the monthly amount in €?

- What are the totals for my monthly income and expenditure?

- How much is available each month? (excess or shortfall?)

Procedure for creating a financial status (part 2 assets/debts):

1. From your asset overview or overview of current debts transfer the figures and important information to the financial status.

2. If necessary, combine individual items in categories.

3. Calculate totals for assets and debts.

4. Ascertain what your net assets are worth or if you are even heavily indebted.

What you can see here:

- What assets do I have and what kind of debts?

- What is the current value (amount) in €?

- What are my total assets worth and
  what is the amount of my total debts in €?

- What are my net assets worth?

- Am I heavily indebted?

Example for creating a financial status:

Player's name:

CASH =
6 x monthly costs
and debts paid off

HAMSTER

RAD

time-account

EGO & BONUS

INCOME

wage/salary	€2,000
further job	
real estate	
business	
securities	
monthly income	**€2,000**

Expenditure

rent/ extra expenses	€600
daily living costs	€600
mortgage	
instalment for car loan	€250
consumer credit	€200
credit card instalment	€140
other expenditure	
child maintenance	
monthly costs	**€1,790**

ASSETS

real estate	
business	
securities	
Liquid assets (CASH)	€3,000
total assets	**€3,000**

DEBTS

mortgage		
car loan	9.5 %	€3,200
consumer credit	12.5 %	€2,700
credit cards	16.8 %	€2,100
account overdraft		
total debts		**€8,000**

Net value - €5,000

Available per month + €210

"Reading" your financial status –

Correctly assess the situation –

Recognise opportunities!

What is the financial situation?

- An income of €2,000 is sufficient to pay ongoing expenses of €1,790.

- €210 per month remains.

- €590 has to go to pay off debt every month;
  this is 33% of the total expenditure!

- €3,000 liquid reserves (cash)

- €8,000 debt level

- Net value - €5.000! There is over-indebtedness!

Are there problems?

- 33% of total expenditure goes to pay off consumer credits.

- The credits have very high interest rates!

- There is over-indebtedness.

- Only one income is available.

What possibilities are there?

Pay back credit card debts with liquid funds with the following consequences:

- Debt reduced by €2,100

- Expenditure reduced by €140/month

- An extra €140 per month available

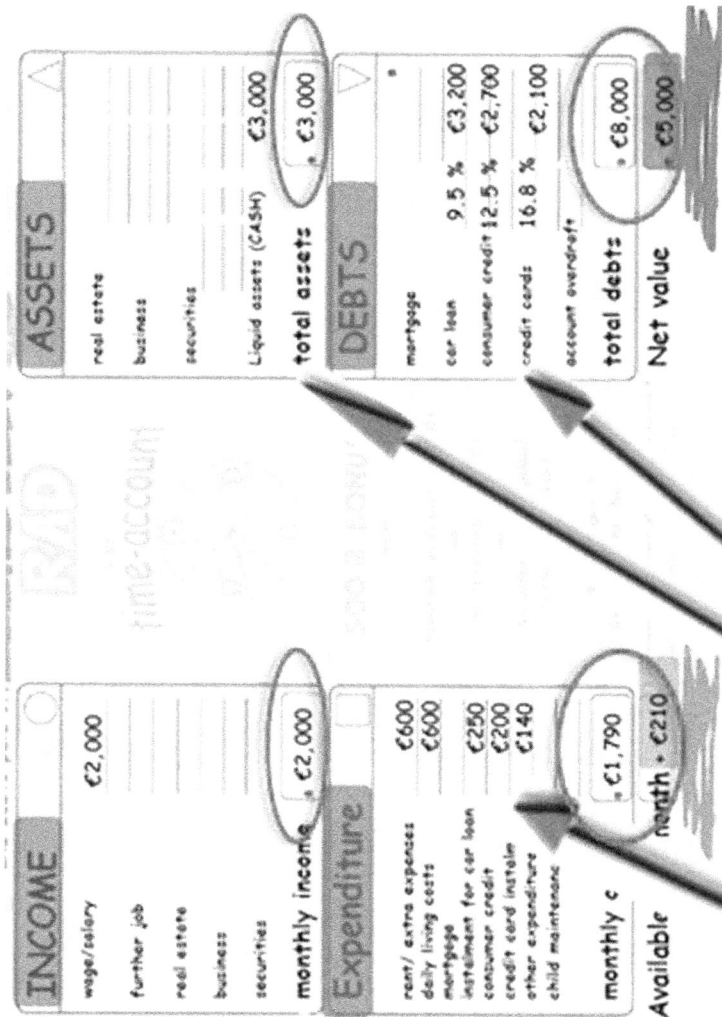

Examine opportunities for taking on an additional job to pay off loans more quickly!

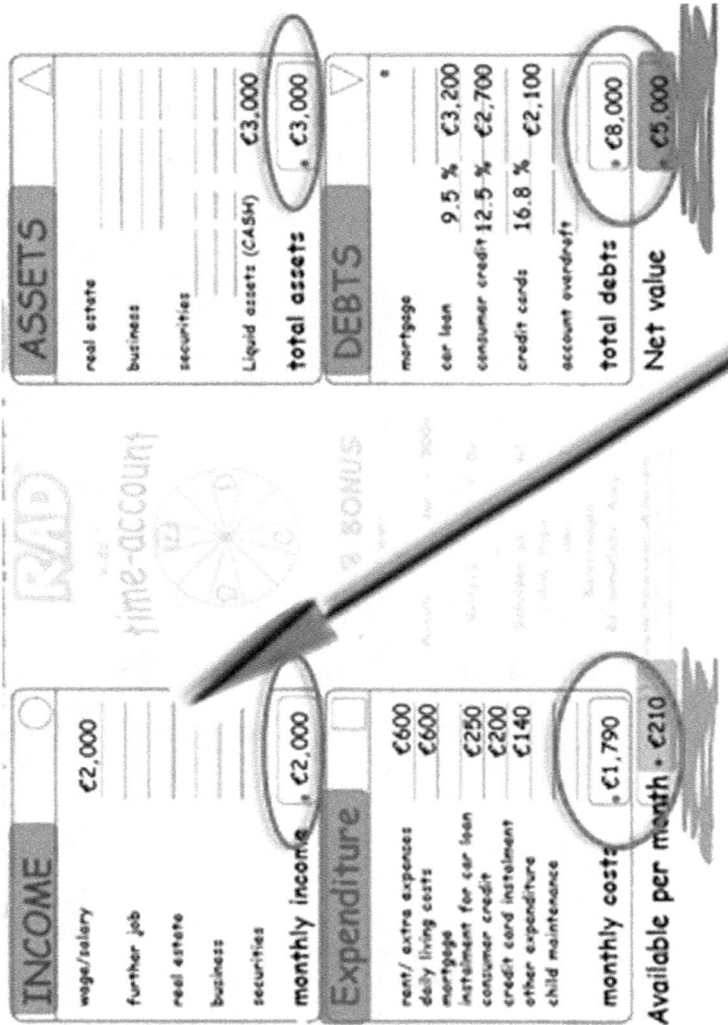

ASSETS

real estate	
business	
securities	
Liquid assets (CASH)	€3,000
total assets	**€3,000**

DEBTS

mortgage		
car loan	9.5 %	€3,200
consumer credit	12.5 %	€2,700
credit cards	16.8 %	€2,100
account overdraft		
total debts		**€8,000**
Net value		**€5,000**

INCOME

wage/salary	€2,000
further job	
real estate	
business	
securities	
monthly income	**€2,000**

Expenditure

rent / extra expenses	€600
daily living costs	€600
mortgage	
instalment for car loan	€250
consumer credit	€200
credit card instalment	€140
other expenditure	
child maintenance	
monthly costs	**€1,790**
Available per month	**€210**

RAD
time-account
BONUS

Negotiate better terms with creditors!

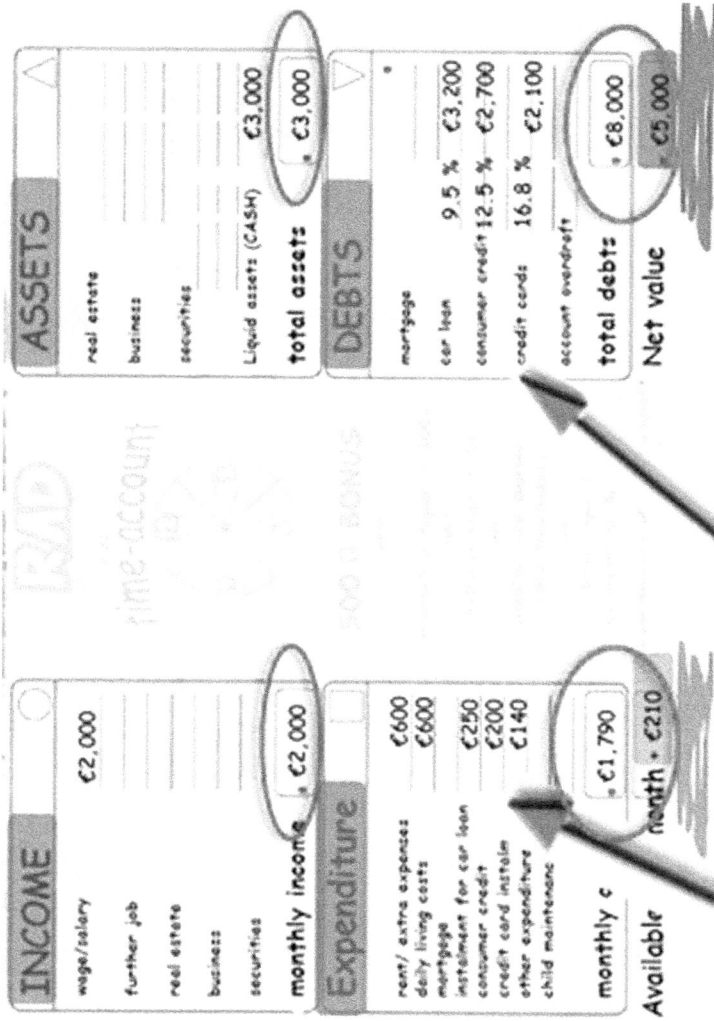

ASSETS

real estate	
business	
securities	
Liquid assets (CASH)	€3,000
total assets	= €3,000

DEBTS

mortgage		
car loan	9.5 %	€3,200
consumer credit	12.5 %	€2,700
credit cards	16.8 %	€2,100
account overdraft		
total debts		= €8,000
Net value		= €5,000

INCOME

wage/salary	€2,000
further job	
real estate	
business	
securities	
monthly income	= €2,000

Expenditure

rent/ extra expenses	€600
daily living costs	€600
mortgage	
instalment for car loan	€250
consumer credit	€200
credit card instalm	€140
other expenditure	
child maintenance	
monthly e	= €1,790
Available	month = €210

NOTES on my financial status:

Where is there an urgent need to take action? What will I do?

My calculations:

My notes:

9 ACTION

ON DECEMBER 31ST WE LIKE TO RAISE A GLASS with family and friends to the New Year and wish one another happiness, satisfaction and success. The telephone lines are then regularly completely overloaded. You want the best for your loved ones and it does good to tell them so. Astrology, horoscopes and lucky charms enjoy a boom as many people expectantly ask what the stars will bring.

Everything should be better in the New Year! Lose weight, do more sport, spend more time with the family, more money. And indeed, at the beginning of the New Year some people start ambitiously working towards the goals they have set themselves. They try losing weight, start jogging, sort papers, tidy up or start an important project. But after a few weeks of hectic activity the daily routine sets in again and with it the old habits. But the next new year is sure to come - sometime. Hope is the last to die!

Make great plans, but don't make the mistake of immediately expecting dramatic changes or even miracles. That would be unhealthy and would only pressure you to demonstrate quick success – to yourself and to others. A journey of a thousand miles starts with the first step, but you need determination, perseverance, flexibility and patience to reach your goal. When planning, you should also set yourself smaller short-term goals. Achieving them has a motivating effect and spurs you on. This confirms that you have chosen the right course.

When you formulate goals write down what you want and not what you don't want!

N.B.: If you just focus on what you don't want, your thoughts and actions will only revolve around the problem. Concentrate on the solution and not on the problem! You will get what you give your mind to consume!

Now is the best time to start! Deep inside everyone knows what is to be done now. But too many people act as a reaction to external influences. Not many have a plan to organise their activities. If you feel pressured or stressed, leave the current situation, calm your emotions, do something you enjoy and take some time to think. Act calmly, sensibly, effectively and in a focused way.

Even a journey of a thousand miles starts with the first step, but you need determination, perseverance, flexibility and patience to reach the goal victoriously!

Fortune is when preparation and opportunity come together. Visible positive changes will come to pass in the course of time, this is bound to happen. Others might think what luck you have had. But for you it will be a confirmation that the right way of thinking, writing things down in a structured manner and focussed action prepared the ground for attracting favourable opportunities. Being happy isn't a pre-determined character trait or an external influence brought about by fate – it is a decision that anyone can make for themselves!

In the final section you sum up all tasks and ideas for action that have been laid down so far at the end of each section. If a topic or a task appears several times it shows how urgent it is. Formulate your goals clearly and without ambiguity and allow yourself to be guided and motivated by a picture of the ideal situation. Set priorities and decide by when you want to achieve the individual results. Record positive results and the date of achieving goals. Look back at your progress and your development and congratulate yourself on what you have achieved. What are you waiting for? Get started!

Life is constant change! Security is an illusion!

…but everything is in the process of constantly improving!

At the beginning of a new idea lots of people know exactly why it doomed to fail.

When an individual allows a utopia to become reality, it becomes normality for many people.

When it has been accomplished everyone is a smart aleck and lots of people had known it since always.

All that we can do now is

to give a little more than the best we are capable at this moment,

to meet new challenges with confidence and passion,

to accept constant changes with trust and

to keep trying to create the prerequisites for a fulfilled, happy and prosperous life for ourselves and for others.

Task Journal

An overview of my important goals

Now summarise all tasks and ideas for action which were identified at the end of the individual sections and categorise similar goals.

- Formulate your goals in a positive, clear and motivating way.

- (What do you want to achieve? Why?)

- Set priorities!

- Set a date for achieving the result.

- Make a note of positive progress and when the goal was achieved.

Task 1	What do I want to do? What do I want to achieve?	By date?	Priority
Goal realised! Date:			
Task 2	What do I want to do? What do I want to achieve?	By date?	Priority
Goal realised! Date:			
Task 3	What do I want to do? What do I want to achieve?	By date?	Priority

The best plan is worthless if it is not realised successfully!

NOTAS sobre la sección de Acción:

Where is there an urgent need to take action? What will I do?

My calculations:

My notes:

ENCLOSURES

*We are thirsty for knowledge but
we are drowning in information.*

Blank templates suitable for your everyday use

Here you will find blank templates suitable for everyday use, to make notes about your situation. Right now, wherever you are!

- Expenditure journal for your wallet

- Expenditure overview (monthly)

- Income overview (monthly)

- My debt cancellation plan

- My purchases/wishes/investments

- BUDGET

- Financial status from the HAMSTERRAD® game

- Task Journal

- Brief information on the HAMSTERRAD® game

- Brief information on the game workshop

Expenditure journal for your wallet

My expenditure

Date	Amount	What	Payment method	Priority

Priorities: A = necessary, B = important, C = pleasant, D = unnecessary

My expenditure

Date	Amount	What	Payment method	Priority

Priorities: A = necessary, B = important, C = pleasant, D = unnecessary

copy templates
Taschengeld Management Der nächste Schritt!®

Expenditure overview (monthly)

EXPENDITURE	Spent each month so far	Annual, urgent, extraordinary needs	Monthly budget	Priority
Total expenditure/month				

copy templates
Taschengeld Management Der nächste Schritt®

Income overview (monthly)

INCOME	Current monthly earnings	Special payments, bonus etc.	Monthly budget	Secure income?
Total income month				

copy templates
Taschengeld Management® Der nächste Schritt! ®

My debt cancellation plan

What debt? creditor	Current amount	Current rate of interest	Minimum installment /month	No. of installments /month	Offer from creditor	Rate of interest new	Installment /month new	No. of installments /month new	Order of priority
Debts/ monthly payments									

copy templates
Taschengeld Management Der nächste Schritt!®

My purchases/wishes/investments

WISHES/PURCHASES/INVESTMENTS	How expensive?	When?	Monthly amount to be saved:	Necessary ?
Monthly reserves for purchases/investments:				

copy templates
Taschengeld Management Der nächste Schritt! ®

Budget

Budget	Monthly	Annually	Excess/ Shortfall	Jan	Feb	Mar	Apr	May	Jun	Jul	Aug	Sep	Oct	Nov	Dec
Private expenditure															
Rent (including heating)															
Additional expenses															
Electricity															
Child maintenance															
Repayment															
Food															
Clothing															
Hairdresser															
Tel / mobile															
Liability insurance															
Total private expenditure															
Debts															
Car purchase															
Overdraft charges															
Bedroom															
Credit card															
Total debts															
Total income - debts															
Income															
Employment															
Holiday pay															
Christmas bonus															
Child benefit															
Total income															
TOTAL: income-expenditure -debts															

Financial status from the HAMSTERRAD® game

Player's name:

CASH MONEY =
6 × monthly costs
and debts paid off

HAMSTER RAD®

INCOME

- wage/salary
- further job
- real estate
- business
- securities

monthly income

Expenditure

- rent/ extra expenses
- daily living costs
- mortgage
- instalment for car loan
- consumer credit
- credit card instalment
- other expenditure
- child maintenance

monthly costs

Available per month

kids:

time-account

500 € BONUS

wenn :

- Monatlich verfügbar > 500€
  oder
- Netto-Vermögen > 0€
  oder
- Schulden sind abgebaut
  (ohne Hypotheken)
  oder
- Barvermögen >
  6x monatliche Ausgaben

ASSETS

- real estate
- business
- securities
- Liquid assets (CASH)

total assets

DEBTS

- mortgage
- car loan
- consumer credit
- credit cards
- account overdraft

total debts

Net value

copy templates

Taschengeld Management Der nächste Schritt! ®

Task Journal

Task	What do I want to do?	By	Priority
	What do I want to achieve?	date?	

Goal realised! Date:

Task	What do I want to do?	By	Priority
	What do I want to achieve?	date?	

Goal realised! Date:

Task	What do I want to do?	By	Priority
	What do I want to achieve?	date?	

Goal realised! Date:

Task	What do I want to do?	By	Priority
	What do I want to achieve?	date?	

Goal realised! Date:

Task	What do I want to do?	By	Priority
	What do I want to achieve?	date?	

Goal realised! Date:

Task	What do I want to do?	By	Priority
	What do I want to achieve?	date?	

Goal realised! Date:

Task	What do I want to do?	By	Priority
	What do I want to achieve?	date?	

Goal realised! Date:

copy templates — Taschengeld Management Der nächste Schritt ®

Brief information on the HAMSTERRAD® game

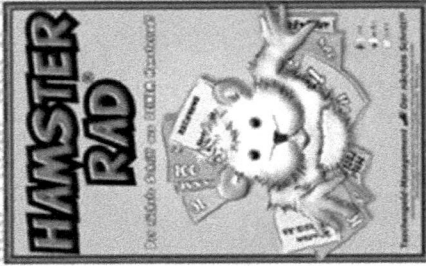

Experience in a game –
Talk with each other –
Learn from each other

About the game HAMSTERRAD®

HAMSTERRAD® is a realistic parlour game that teaches good money management in a fun way. You experience everyday financial problems such as rising costs, oppressive debts, a lack of reserves, reduced working hours or even job loss and must master them.

The player wins who pays off his or her debts first and saves 6x his or her monthly expenditure.

In the game the players experience daily challenges relating to money, exchange experiences and learn from one another.

Order (German version) from www.hamsterrad.info

In 2010 HAMSTERRAD® was nominated for the German educational game prize!

Brief information on the game workshop

PLAYING = PRACTICE FOR DAILY LIFE!

HAMSTERRAD® simulates financial reality.

Financial decisions and possible consequences are tried out.

Without actually investing money, knowledge and lots of practical experience are imparted in a short space of time.

The game enables learning in a motivating and creative environment.

Each roll of the dice calls for intelligent decisions in order to master new financial challenges.

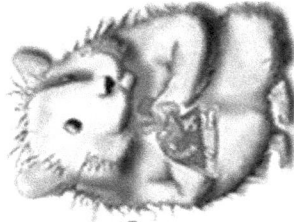

Further information on the game workshop (held in Germany) is available at www.taschengeld-management.de

EXPERIENCE - LEARN - DISCOVER

About the game workshop

ABOUT THE AUTHOR

Walter Berger is an author, game inventor, founder and owner of Taschengeld Management, a private initiative for the economic consumer education.

"With our offer, we want to help everyone, in a practical and comprehensible way to gain orientation and overview in everyday finances. Everyone should be qualified to make "right" decisions. This is an important prerequisite and motivation to meaningful actions!"

Walter Berger
Taschengeld Management
Florianiplatz 16
83435 Bad Reichenhall, Deutschland

www.taschengeld-management.de
info@taschengeld-management.de